THE POWER OF CONNECTIONS: A MENTEE'S GUIDE TO NETWORKING MASTERY

The Essential Networking Playbook

JANAYA HERNANDEZ

Copyright © 2024 by Janaya Hernandez

All rights reserved.

THE POWER OF CONNECTIONS: A MENTEE'S GUIDE TO NETWORKING MASTERY

In today's fast-paced world, the ability to forge meaningful connections can be the defining factor between success and stagnation. "The Power of Connections" is not just a guide; it's your roadmap to mastering the art of networking as a mentee. Whether you are just starting your career journey or seeking to elevate your professional presence, this book will equip you with the tools, strategies, and insights needed to cultivate lasting relationships that open doors and create opportunities.

Imagine walking into a room filled with potential—each person you meet is a chance to learn, grow, and collaborate. With the right approach, networking transforms from a daunting task into an exciting adventure. This book will empower you to harness your unique strengths, embrace vulnerability, and confidently engage with mentors, peers, and industry leaders.

As you turn these pages, you will discover:
- The essential principles of effective networking
- Proven techniques to build rapport and trust
- Strategies for leveraging connections to navigate your career path
- Real-life stories and insights from successful professionals who have mastered the art of networking

Prepare to embark on a transformative journey where every connection counts. Together, let's unlock the true potential of your networking endeavors and turn fleeting encounters into powerful partnerships. Welcome to "The Power of Connections"—where your networking mastery begins!

"Your network is your net worth"
-Porter Gale

CONTENTS

Introduction ix
  1. Networking Basics 1
  2. The Power of Communication 25
  3. Expanding Your Network 43
  4. Online networking 49
  5. Mastering the Art of Follow-Up 55
  6. Networking with Purpose 61
  7. Networking Etiquette and Best Practices 65
  8. Giving and Receiving Referrals 71
  9. Networking in Diversity and Inclusion 81
10. Networking for Career Growth 91
Conclusion 97

INTRODUCTION

Welcome to the exciting world of networking, conferences, and sponsorship. In today's professional landscape, building a strong network and making meaningful connections can open doors to endless opportunities. Whether you are an aspiring professional, an entrepreneur, or a seasoned industry expert, mastering the art of networking is essential for success.

In this book, we will explore the ins and outs of networking, delve into the power of conferences, and uncover the benefits of sponsorship. We will guide you through the process of building and expanding your network, nurturing relationships, and leveraging your connections for career advancement and personal growth.

Networking may seem intimidating or overwhelming, but fear not! We will provide you with practical tips, strategies, and real-life examples to help you navigate networking events, make lasting impressions, and create a network that truly supports your goals.

Conferences offer a unique platform for networking, learning, and showcasing your expertise. We will equip you with the knowledge to choose the right conferences, prepare effectively, and maximize the networking opportunities they present. You'll discover how conferences can become a catalyst for professional growth and development.

Sponsorship, on the other hand, can provide a significant boost to your networking efforts. We will explore different types of sponsorship and guide you through the process of securing sponsorship opportunities. You'll learn how to leverage sponsorships to enhance your credibility, visibility, and networking potential.

Throughout this book, we will address common networking challenges, such as social anxiety, introversion, and handling rejection. We believe that networking is a skill that can be learned and honed, regardless of personality type or experience level. By the end of this book, you'll be equipped with the tools and confidence to network effectively in any setting.

So, whether you're attending a conference, seeking sponsorship, or simply looking to expand your network, let's embark on this networking journey together. It's time to unlock the power of networking, seize new opportunities, and elevate your professional and personal life.

CHAPTER 1
NETWORKING BASICS

Networking is more than just exchanging business cards or attending social events; it is about building genuine connections and meaningful relationships. In this chapter, we will lay the foundation for effective networking by exploring the fundamental principles and strategies that will set you on the path to success.

Networking is a powerful tool that goes beyond simple exchanges and social events. It is about creating authentic connections and meaningful relationships. Establishing the groundwork for effective networking by delving into the core principles and strategies will help guide you towards success.

Understanding the Importance of Networking: Lets deep dive in a discuss, why networking is crucial in both personal and professional settings. . Networking is not just a professional necessity but a vital aspect of personal growth. The relationships you build can lead to numerous opportunities, enriching both your personal and professional life. By actively engaging in networking, you position yourself for success and ensure that you are never alone in your journey. Building relationships with key decision-makers can increase your visibility within your organization, potentially leading to promotions and advancements.

Networking opens doors to opportunities, helps you build a support system, and enhances your visibility and reputation, where one can establish and build nurturing relationships with individuals who can provide support, information, and opportunities. This can occur in formal settings, such as conferences and seminars, or informally, through social gatherings and online platforms. A strong network can act as a safety net, providing emotional and professional support during challenging times. Engaging with diverse groups can expose you to new ideas, perspectives, and skills, fostering personal growth. Many job openings and business deals are filled through referrals and word-of-mouth. Networking can lead to job offers and partnerships that may not be advertised publicly. Being active in your field helps you establish a presence. The more you connect with others, the more likely you are to be recognized as a knowledgeable professional.

Approach networking with a genuine interest in others. Authentic relationships are more valuable than superficial connections Platforms like LinkedIn offer opportunities to connect with professionals globally. Share valuable content and engage in discussions to enhance your online presence. Understand that not every connection will lead to immediate results. Approach networking as a long-term investment in your career. After meeting someone, follow up with a message or email. Identify what you want to achieve through networking—whether it's finding a mentor, seeking job opportunities, or expanding your knowledge in a particular area.

Take Sara for example , A young woman named Sarah from Manhattan looking to elevate her career to the next level. Sara had been at her current position and being looked over for 9 years. She very rarely interacted with her coworkers , or expanded outside of her department. Extremely tired of being passed on promotion she decided to connect with a member on the leadership team in hopes to receive feedback and mentorship. Mark, a seasoned marketing director who had once walked the same path she was on provided Sara with some useful insight. Mark had navigated his own journey through the maze of networking. "It's not just about what you know," he said. "It's about who you know—and how you nurture those connections." Sarah took Mark's advice to heart. She began networking and making genuine connections throughout her organization . She started with Mark . She made it a point to follow up with him on LinkedIn, and taking him up on his offer to do social networking. Over the months, they exchanged insights about the industry, and Mark became a mentor, guiding her through challenges and celebrating her successes.

As Sarah's confidence grew, so did her network. She began attending industry workshops, where she met professionals from various backgrounds. Each connection was a thread in her expanding web—some became friends, others collaborators, and a few even turned into job leads. At one event, she met Lisa, a healthcare administrator at successful hospital, who was looking for a Practice Manager for a new location. Together, they brainstormed ideas and soon launched a successful opening of the new location that garnered attention from upper leadership.

Networking wasn't always easy for Sarah. At times, she felt overwhelmed by the sheer number of people in the room, and the fear of rejection loomed large. But she remembered Mark's words: "Every connection is a potential opportunity, and every conversation has the power to change your trajectory." Embracing this mindset, Sarah approached each networking opportunity with success.

Networking isn't just about climbing the corporate ladder, nor is it just about what you can gain; it's also about what you can contribute. By being a resource for others and nurturing those relationships, you'll create a network that is mutually beneficial and enduring, which will start to building a community. Embrace networking as a lifelong skill—one that would not only open doors to opportunities but also weave a tapestry of relationships that would last a lifetime. The more you invest in others, the richer your network becomes. It's a web of connections that can support you through every twist and turn of your journey.

You have to be realistic that challenges will occur. Remember Sara didn't always feel confident and successful. Remember a goal without a plan is just a wish. Taking a proactive approach to networking efforts should help overcoming common networking challenges. Mapping your networking journey will result in a successful outcome.

Networking is not just about expanding your contacts; it's about intentional connections that align with your aspirations, When you set clear goals, you create a path that leads you to your desired destination. Create an Action Plan: Once you have defined your networking goals, create an action plan to guide your networking activities. Break down your goals into smaller, actionable steps. For example, if your goal is to attend industry events, your action plan could include researching upcoming events, registering for them, and preparing a list of people you want to connect with.

YOUR NETWORKING GOAL-SETTING ACTION PLAN

As you embark on your own networking journey, consider these actionable steps:
1. Define your networking objectives and identify their purpose.
2. Use the SMART criteria to create specific and measurable goals.
3. Develop a networking plan with prioritized connections and milestones.
4. Regularly review and adjust your goals as needed, celebrating your progress along the way.

DEFINING YOUR NETWORKING GOALS

To make the most out of networking, it's important to set clear goals and objectives. Whether it's expanding your professional circle, finding job opportunities, or seeking industry insights. Having well-defined goals will help you focus your networking efforts and make them more purposeful. Defining your networking goals is crucial for making your networking efforts more purposeful and effective.

Setting Networking Goals: By defining your objectives, you can focus your efforts and make the most of your networking opportunities.

- Develop a networking mindset: This includes being open-minded, approachable, and genuinely interested in others. Also identify what common networking fears you have and devise a plan on how to overcome them.

- Build and maintain relationships: Develop a natural art of building and nurturing relationships. From making a positive first impression to maintaining regular contact, to fostering genuine connections with your network.
- Effective communication: This includes active listening, asking thoughtful questions, and conveying your message clearly and confidently.
- Networking Etiquette: Understanding and practicing proper etiquette will help you navigate networking events with confidence and professionalism.

By understanding and implementing these networking basics, you will lay a solid foundation for successful networking and pave the way for meaningful connections and opportunities in your personal and professional life. Keep yourself accountable, like Sara establish milestones. By the end of each month, review your progress, take note of the connections you've made and the conversations initiated. An important note to add would be to celebrate achievements:

Evaluate and Adjust. Regularly evaluate your progress towards your networking goals and make adjustments as needed. Assess what is working well and what needs improvement. Be open to adapting your approach based on your experiences and feedback from your network. Our friend Sarah celebrated each milestone, no matter how small. Whether it was securing a mentorship meeting or receiving helpful advice, acknowledging her successes motivated her to keep pushing forward. This allows reflection to transpire. Looking back on your journey, will give you a better understanding that setting networking goals with a clear roadmap, can turn networking from a daunting task into an exciting adventure filled with opportunities.

Reflect on Your Objectives, Start by reflecting on what you hope to achieve through networking. Consider both your short-term and long-term goals. Are you looking to expand your professional network, find job opportunities, gain industry insights, or seek mentorship? Understanding your objectives will help you set specific goals. Be Specific and Measurable: When setting networking goals, it's important to be specific and measurable. Instead of setting a vague goal like "network more," consider setting goals such as "attend at least two industry events per month" or "connect with five new professionals in my field each week." Having specific and measurable goals allows you to track your progress and evaluate your networking efforts. If you have multiple networking goals, prioritize them based on their importance and relevance to your current situation. This will help you allocate your time and resources effectively. Consider which goals will have the most significant impact on your personal and professional growth.

While it's important to have networking goals, it's also essential to maintain a balance. Networking should not be a transactional activity focused solely on what you can gain. Building genuine relationships and offering support to others should also be a part of your networking approach. By defining your networking goals, you can focus your efforts, make meaningful connections, and maximize the benefits of networking. Remember to regularly review and update your goals as your needs and circumstances change.

UNDERSTANDING THE POWER OF NETWORKING

Networking is a powerful tool that can open doors to new opportunities, career growth, and personal development. Using Sara's experience as an example illustrates a picture of the benefits of networking, including access to knowledge, resources, mentorship, and collaboration. Understanding the true value of networking will motivate and inspire you to invest time and effort into building your network.

Here are some key points to understand about the power of networking:

Access to Knowledge and Information: Networking allows you to connect with individuals from diverse backgrounds and industries. By engaging in conversations and building relationships, you gain access to valuable knowledge and information. You can learn about industry trends, best practices, and gain insights that can help you make informed decisions and stay ahead of the curve.

Alex's unlike Sara had to really enagae in the power of connecting with individulas from a diverse background. Alex belong to many networking organization such as The American College of Healthcare Exuctives , and was currently in a leadership role. His organization however did not provide a diversify leadership panel, and he struggle to connect with his current team and lack guidance from his superiors. Through his outside networking groups Alex gained the power of knowledge exchange and brought back to his organization how diversifying your network can help overcome important challenge within the organization.

Its was at these networking events that Alex made a conscious effort to engage with as many people as he could. Approaching non- similar group discussing the latest challenges across healthcare and participating in learning in a non-typical environment. Alex realized that every person represented a unique perspective, a different experience, and a wealth of knowledge just waiting to be discovered.

Keep in mind that Networking is not just about who you know; it's about the wisdom they share. Every connection can teach you something invaluable—be it a new approach to problem-solving or insights into changes.

Networking had become a gateway to continuous learning. The relationships you build are not just about professional gain; they are a source of wisdom that brings enrichment to understanding of the industry. Knowledge is a treasure that grows when shared. she Through networking, we tap into a collective intelligence that keeps us ahead of the curve.

As you embark on your networking journey, consider these actionable steps to tap into the wealth of knowledge available:

1. **Be Curious:** Approach conversations with a genuine interest in learning from others.
2. **Ask Open-Ended Questions:** Encourage deeper discussions that reveal insights and best practices.
3. **Share Your Own Knowledge:** Contribute to the conversation by sharing your experiences and expertise.
4. **Create Knowledge Sharing Opportunities:** Organize gatherings or online discussions that facilitate the exchange of ideas among your network.

Networking opens up opportunities for resource sharing and collaboration. When you build a strong network, you have a pool of contacts who can provide support, advice, and guidance. Whether you need assistance with a project, access to a specific skill set, or recommendations for service providers, your network can be a valuable resource. Allowing you to connect with experienced professionals who can serve as mentors and guides. These mentors can offer valuable advice, share their experiences, and provide guidance on navigating your career or personal challenges. Having a mentor within your network can accelerate your growth and help you avoid common pitfalls. By Alex looking for guidance outside of his organization he was able to tap into a diverse panel of experience professional and bring those lessons back to his organization.

Building a strong diverse network helps you establish a positive reputation and increase your visibility within your industry or community. When you consistently engage with others, contribute value, and build meaningful connections, your name becomes associated with credibility and expertise. This can lead to invitations for speaking engagements, collaborations, and other opportunities to showcase your skills and knowledge.

Networking provides you with a support system of like-minded individuals who understand the challenges and triumphs you face. Being part of a supportive network can offer emotional support, motivation, and encouragement during tough times. Your network can also celebrate your successes and provide a sense of belonging.

BUILDING YOUR NETWORKING MINDSET

Networking requires a positive and proactive mindset. The mindset shifts is necessary to become a successful networker, including overcoming self-doubt, embracing a growth mindset, and cultivating a genuine desire to help others. Developing the right mindset will pave the way for authentic and meaningful connections.

Building the right mindset is crucial for becoming a successful networker. Here are some mindset shifts to consider:

- One of the first mindset shifts is overcoming self-doubt. Many people feel hesitant or insecure when networking, fearing rejection or feeling like an imposter. Recognize that everyone has unique strengths and experiences to offer. Focus on your own value and what you bring to the table. Embrace the belief that you have something valuable to contribute to conversations and relationships.

- Embracing a Growth Mindset, Adopting a growth mindset is essential for continuous learning and growth in networking. Understand that networking is not just about immediate outcomes, but also about personal and professional development. Embrace challenges as opportunities for learning, view setbacks as temporary, and believe in your ability to improve and adapt. With a growth mindset, you'll be more open to new experiences and willing to step out of your comfort zone.
- Cultivating a Genuine Desire to Help Others, Networking is not just about what you can gain, but also about how you can contribute and support others. Cultivate a genuine desire to help others and build mutually beneficial relationships. Approach networking with a mindset of generosity and curiosity. Ask questions, actively listen, and offer assistance when possible. When you focus on building meaningful connections and adding value to others, you create a positive networking environment.
- Confidence plays a significant role in networking. Build your confidence by preparing and practicing beforehand. Research the people you want to connect with, be knowledgeable about current industry trends, and have an elevator pitch ready to introduce yourself. Remember that confidence comes with experience, so the more you network, the more comfortable and confident you will become.

- Authenticity is key to building genuine connections. Be yourself and let your personality shine through in your interactions. Avoid trying to be someone you're not or using scripted conversations. Authenticity establishes trust and makes it easier for others to connect with you on a deeper level.
- Networking can sometimes be challenging, but maintaining a positive attitude is essential. Approach networking with enthusiasm and optimism. Be open to new opportunities and perspectives. Even if things don't go as planned, view setbacks as learning experiences and keep moving forward.

By embracing these mindset shifts, you can develop a positive and proactive networking mindset. Remember that building meaningful connections takes time and effort. Be patient, persistent, and genuine in your networking endeavors.

DEVELOPING YOUR PERSONAL BRAND

Your personal brand is a reflection of your professional identity and what you bring to the table. We will discuss the importance of developing a strong personal brand and how it can enhance your networking efforts. We will delve into crafting an elevator pitch, optimizing your online presence, and leveraging your unique strengths and skills.

Developing a strong personal brand is crucial for standing out in the professional world and making meaningful connections. Here are some key aspects to consider when developing your personal brand:

- Define Your Unique Value Proposition: Start by identifying your unique strengths, skills, and experiences. What sets you apart from others in your field? What value do you bring to the table? This is your unique value proposition. Understanding and articulating your strengths will help you effectively communicate your personal brand to others.
- Craft an Elevator Pitch: An elevator pitch is a concise and compelling summary of who you are, what you do, and what value you offer. It should be brief enough to deliver in the time it takes to ride an elevator (around 30-60 seconds). Your elevator pitch should highlight your unique value proposition and leave a lasting impression on the listener. Practice and refine your elevator pitch to make it clear, concise, and impactful.
- Optimize Your Online Presence: In today's digital age, your online presence plays a significant role in shaping your personal brand. Ensure that your social media profiles, website (if applicable), and professional platforms like LinkedIn are up-to-date and aligned with your personal brand. Use consistent branding elements, such as a professional profile photo and a consistent tone of voice. Share relevant content, showcase your expertise, and engage with others in your industry to build credibility and visibility.
- Leverage Your Unique Strengths and Skills: Identify your key strengths and skills and find ways to leverage them in your networking efforts. For example, if you're a great

communicator, focus on building relationships through meaningful conversations. If you have expertise in a specific area, position yourself as a resource or thought leader in that field. By highlighting and utilizing your unique strengths and skills, you can differentiate yourself and attract like-minded professionals.

- Be Authentic and Consistent: Authenticity is crucial in building a strong personal brand. Be true to yourself and let your genuine personality shine through in your interactions. Consistency is also important. Ensure that your personal brand is consistent across all platforms and interactions. This creates a cohesive and memorable impression on others.
- Seek Feedback and Adapt: Regularly seek feedback from trusted mentors, colleagues, or networking contacts. Ask for their perception of your personal brand and how you can improve. Be open to constructive criticism and use it as an opportunity to refine and adapt your personal brand as needed.

Going back to Sara's mentor Mark and the tools he provided Sara regarding the importance of seeking feedback while showcasing Sarah's evolution in her personal networking journey. He focused on a very valuable tool called "Setting the Scene & Growing Ambition". As Sarah settled into her new found confidence making valuable connections and gaining insights from her networking experiences, Mark expressed that she truly find a way to stand out, she needed to refine her personal brand. Your brand is like a story, It should reflect who you are, what you stand for, and how you can uniquely contribute to the world. Feedback is the cornerstone of growth, You should regularly seek input from trusted mentors and colleagues. Their perspectives can illuminate blind spots and reveal opportunities for improvement.

WHAT DO YOU WANT PEOPLE TO ASSOCIATE WITH YOUR NAME?

It's human nature to shy away from showcasing your successes. You have to own your achievements to build your brand. Peer with a mentor to develop a personal branding strategy that includes:

- Define your core values which would serve as the foundation of your brand.
- Enhancing online presence . Ensure that your online presence aligns with your values and aspirations. Craft a compelling bio that highlights your unique skills and experiences.
- Showcase your achievements. Learn to celebrate your successes and articulate your contributions.

As you implement these changes, you will notice a shift in how people respond. Remember "Networking with Purpose". Your brand is a living entity, It evolves as you do, so seeking feedback and adapting is essential for growth." Seeking feedback had not only refines your personal brand but also provides a more confident and self-aware professional. Feedback is a gift, It's an opportunity to evolve and adapt, ensuring that our personal brands resonate with our true selves.

As you embark on your journey of personal branding, remember these actionable steps:

- Seek Feedback: Regularly ask trusted mentors, colleagues, and networking contacts for their perceptions of your brand.
- Be Open: Embrace constructive criticism and view it as a chance for growth.
- Reflect and Adapt: Use the insights gained to refine your personal brand, aligning it with your goals and values.
- Maintain Connections: Schedule regular check-ins with mentors to discuss your progress and continue receiving guidance.

Remember, developing a personal brand is an ongoing process. It requires self-reflection, continuous learning, and intentional effort. By crafting a compelling elevator pitch, optimizing your online presence, and leveraging your unique strengths, you can develop a strong personal brand that enhances your networking efforts and opens doors to new opportunities.

BUILDING AND EXPANDING YOUR NETWORK

Growing your network is an ongoing process. Building off practical strategies for building and expanding your network, including attending networking events, leveraging social media platforms, and engaging in professional communities can at first be overwhelming. Building and expanding your professional network is essential for career growth and opportunities. Attending industry conferences, seminars, workshops, and networking events to connect with like-minded professionals can be a rewarding outcome that pays off in the end. These events provide valuable opportunities to meet new people, exchange ideas, and build relationships. Our diverse leader Alex provides us an outlook on how to navigate this successfully. These events serve as vital opportunities for connection and growth while highlighting the challenges and triumphs.

Alex knew that the path to success in gaining an understanding of diverse leaders laid in expanding his network. He had heard time and again from mentors and peers that attending networking events was essential for connecting with like-minded professionals.

When attending these events Alex made a conscious effort to listen actively and ask questions. "He inquired, genuinely interested in fellow healthcare leaders experiences. This approach helped him establish rapport and foster connections and provided him with the tools and confidence to bring back to his organization.

Networking is not just about making connections; it's about nurturing them. Every conversation opens doors to new opportunities and insights.

As you embark on your networking journey, consider these actionable steps:
1. Attend networking events: Seek out conferences, seminars, and workshops relevant to your field to connect with like-minded professionals.
2. Be Proactive: Introduce yourself to new people, engage in conversations, and share your insights.
3. Follow Up: After the event, send personalized follow-up messages to nurture the connections you made.
4. Build Relationships: Schedule one-on-one meetings or coffee chats to deepen your connections and explore collaboration opportunities.

Leverage Social Media Platforms: Utilize social media platforms like LinkedIn, and Instagram, to expand your professional network. Create a compelling and professional online presence, and actively engage with others in your industry. Join relevant groups and participate in discussions, share content, and connect with professionals who align with your interests and goals. Remember to maintain a professional tone and build genuine connections.

Engage in Professional Communities. Join professional associations, industry-specific groups, and online communities to connect with professionals in your field. Attend their events, participate in forums, and contribute to discussions. By actively engaging in these communities, you can establish yourself as a knowledgeable and valuable member, and build relationships with peers and industry leaders. Offer Help and Support: Building a strong network is not just about what you can gain, but also about what you can give. Offer your assistance, knowledge, and support to others in your network. Share relevant resources, provide feedback, and connect people who may benefit from knowing each other. By being generous and helpful, you build trust and establish yourself as a valuable connection.

Maintain and Nurture Relationships: Building a network is not a one-time activity; it requires ongoing effort. Stay in touch with your connections by sending occasional emails, inviting them for coffee or virtual meetings, and congratulating them on their accomplishments. Show genuine interest in their work and goals. Regularly engage with their content on social media and provide meaningful comments. By nurturing your relationships, you strengthen your network and increase the likelihood of opportunities and referrals.

Seek Mentorship and Guidance: Identify professionals who have achieved success in your desired field and seek their mentorship or guidance. Mentors can provide valuable insights, advice, and support. They can also introduce you to their own network, opening doors to new connections and opportunities. Approach potential mentors with respect and a clear understanding of what you hope to gain from the relationship.

Remember, building and expanding your network takes time and effort. Be proactive, genuine, and consistent in your networking activities. Focus on building meaningful connections, nurturing relationships, and providing value to others. A strong network can support your career goals, provide opportunities for collaboration and learning, and open doors to new possibilities.

NETWORKING ETIQUETTE AND BEST PRACTICES

Networking etiquette plays a crucial role in making a positive impression and building strong relationships. Networking etiquette is essential for making a positive impression and building rapport with others. Mastering these skills will help you navigate networking events with confidence and leave a lasting impression. Elaborating on key networking etiquette tips and best practices, such as active listening, effective communication, and follow-up strategies.

Here are some key networking etiquette tips and best practices to help you navigate networking events with confidence:

- Be Approachable: Maintain an open and friendly demeanor when attending networking events. Smile, make eye contact, and approach others with a welcoming attitude. Avoid appearing distracted or disinterested by putting away your phone and giving your full attention to the conversation.
- Active Listening: Practice active listening by fully engaging in conversations and showing genuine interest in what others have to say. Avoid interrupting or dominating the conversation. Instead, ask thoughtful questions, nod in agreement, and provide verbal and non-verbal cues that demonstrate your attentiveness.
- Effective Communication: Clearly articulate your thoughts and ideas while engaging in conversations. Be mindful of your body language, tone of voice, and choice of words. Maintain a positive and professional demeanor, and avoid

negative or controversial topics. Practice concise and impactful communication to leave a lasting impression.

- Exchange Contact Information: When connecting with someone, exchange contact information in a professional manner. Consider carrying business cards or use digital alternatives like LinkedIn QR codes. Be sure to ask for their preferred method of contact (email, phone, etc.) and follow up promptly after the event to reinforce the connection.
- Follow-Up: Follow up with individuals you meet at networking events to nurture the relationship. Send a personalized email or LinkedIn message within a few days, expressing your gratitude for the conversation and highlighting any specific points you discussed. Mention your interest in staying connected and offer any assistance or resources you may have discussed.
- Networking events can be busy, so be mindful of others' time and commitments. Avoid monopolizing someone's attention for too long and be aware of cues that they may need to move on. Respect personal boundaries and avoid overly assertive or intrusive behavior.
- Networking is a two-way street. Offer assistance, resources, or introductions to others whenever possible. Show genuine interest in their goals and challenges. At the same time, be open to receiving help, advice, and opportunities. Networking is about building mutually beneficial relationships. The goal is to Give and Receive.
- Express your gratitude to event organizers, hosts, and anyone who has made the networking event possible. Send

a thank-you note or email to acknowledge their efforts in organizing and providing the opportunity for professionals to connect.

By following these networking etiquette tips and best practices, you can make a positive impression, build rapport with others, and leave a lasting impact. Networking is about building genuine relationships and adding value to others' professional journeys.

CHAPTER 2
THE POWER OF COMMUNICATION

"A mentor is someone who sees the talent in you and helps you to unleash it." – Unknown

In our fast-paced world, the ability to articulate your ideas clearly and persuasively in a short timeframe can open doors to new opportunities. Just as the elevator pitch distills your value and message into a few impactful sentences, mastering communication requires understanding your audience, engaging with confidence, and adapting your approach to foster meaningful connections.

Mastering communication is essential for both personal and professional success. By understanding the communication process, honing your verbal and nonverbal skills, and adapting to your audience, you can create impactful interactions that foster collaboration and understanding.

With that in mind, let's delve into Chapter 2: "The Power of Communication," where we will uncover the foundational techniques and strategies that will empower you to enhance your communication skills and create lasting impressions in every interaction.

Effective communication is the cornerstone of building relationships, conveying ideas, and achieving goals. Whether in personal interactions, professional settings, or public speaking, mastering communication allows you to express yourself clearly, listen actively, and connect with others on a deeper level. This chapter will explore essential communication skills, techniques, and strategies to enhance your overall effectiveness as a communicator. Different audiences require different approaches.

As we explore the art of effective communication, one essential tool that stands out is the elevator pitch. An elevator pitch is a concise and compelling introduction that communicates who you are, what you do, and what makes you unique. We will guide you through the process of crafting a compelling elevator pitch that showcases your skills and expertise. A well-prepared elevator pitch will help you make a memorable first impression and spark conversations with ease. Engaging in meaningful conversations is at the heart of networking events. Practicing these conversational skills will help you build rapport, establish connections, and make the most out of your networking interactions.

In professional settings, first impressions matter immensely. An elevator pitch is a succinct and compelling introduction that encapsulates who you are, what you do, and what you aim to achieve. Whether you're at a networking event, a job interview, or a casual meet-up, a well-crafted elevator pitch can open doors to opportunities and make you memorable.

Before diving into the crafting process, let's clarify what an elevator pitch entails:

- Concise: Your pitch should be brief, ideally lasting no longer than 30 seconds to a minute—about the time it takes to ride an elevator.
- Compelling: It should capture attention and create interest in what you have to offer.

- Focused: Clearly communicate your professional background, key skills, and goals.

To create an effective elevator pitch, you need to identify the core components that will form the foundation of your introduction.

1. Professional Background: Start by summarizing your current position and relevant experience. Consider including your educational background if it's pertinent.

    Example: "I'm Alex, a digital marketing specialist with over five years of experience in the tech industry."

2. Skills: Highlight your unique skills or areas of expertise that set you apart from others in your field.

    Example: "I specialize in leveraging artificial intelligence to enhance customer engagement and drive marketing strategies."

3. Goals: Conclude with your professional aspirations. This shows your ambition and gives your audience insight into what you hope to achieve.

    Example: "My goal is to revolutionize the marketing landscape by providing innovative solutions that empower brands."

Now that you've identified your key components, it's time to weave them together into a cohesive elevator pitch. Here's a simple formula you can follow:

1. Start with Your Name and Role: Introduce yourself clearly. "Hi, I'm Alex, a digital marketing specialist…"
2. Briefly Describe Your Background: Offer a snapshot of your experience.

    "…with over five years of experience in the tech industry."

3. Highlight Your Skills: Emphasize your unique strengths. "I specialize in leveraging artificial intelligence…"
4. State Your Goals: Share what you aspire to achieve. "…and my goal is to revolutionize the marketing landscape."

Putting it all together, your elevator pitch might sound like this:

"Hi, I'm Alex, a digital marketing specialist with over five years of experience in the tech industry. I specialize in leveraging artificial intelligence to enhance customer engagement and drive marketing strategies. My goal is to revolutionize the marketing landscape by providing innovative solutions that empower brands."

Once you've crafted your pitch, the next step is to practice. Here are some tips to ensure you deliver it confidently:

- Rehearse Aloud: Stand in front of a mirror or record yourself. This helps with pacing and intonation.
- Seek Feedback: Practice in front of friends or colleagues and ask for constructive criticism.
- Adjust for Authenticity: Make sure the pitch feels natural to you. Adjust any language or phrases that don't align with your speaking style.

When the moment comes to share your elevator pitch, remember these key points:

- Be Personable: Approach your introduction with warmth and enthusiasm. A genuine smile can make a lasting impression.
- Maintain Eye Contact: This builds rapport and shows that you are engaged.

- Listen and Engage: Be prepared to continue the conversation. Ask questions and show interest in your audience's responses.

Crafting an effective elevator pitch is a valuable skill that can significantly enhance your networking efforts and professional opportunities. By presenting a clear, concise, and compelling introduction, you set the stage for meaningful conversations and connections.

Action Steps:
- Identify your key components (background, skills, goals).
- Craft your elevator pitch using the provided formula.
- Practice delivering your pitch until it feels natural.
- Use your pitch as a tool to engage others and foster connections.

Effective communication is not merely about exchanging information; it's about creating understanding. It involves verbal and nonverbal elements, context, and the relationship between the communicators. Mastering communication enables you to articulate your thoughts clearly, listen actively, and connect meaningfully with others, fostering collaboration and building strong relationships.

Mastering communication is a lifelong journey that enhances your ability to connect with others, share ideas, and influence outcomes. By understanding the components of communication, honing verbal and nonverbal skills, and adapting to your audience, you empower yourself to engage effectively in any situation.

Starting conversations can be challenging, especially in a networking setting where you may not know many people.

Asking open-ended questions is a powerful way to keep a conversation flowing and show genuine interest in the other person. We will share examples of open-ended questions that can stimulate engaging discussions. By asking thoughtful questions, you'll encourage the other person to share more about themselves, creating a deeper connection.

Here are strategies for adapting your communication style:

Active Listening: Show that you are engaged by nodding, maintaining eye contact, and providing verbal affirmations. It shows engagement through nonverbal cues like nodding and leaning slightly forward. This indicates that you are present and invested in the conversation citing back what you've heard can also ensure understanding.

Active listening is a crucial skill for effective communication. We will discuss techniques for active listening, such as maintaining eye contact, nodding, and summarizing the other person's points. By actively listening, you'll demonstrate your attentiveness and make the other person feel valued and understood. Practice Active Listening: Prepare yourself to actively listen and engage in meaningful conversations. Maintain eye contact, nod in agreement, and show genuine interest in what others are saying. This will help you build connections and leave a positive impression.

In our fast-paced world, where conversations often feel rushed, the true art of communication is often overlooked: active listening. This chapter will guide you through the importance of active listening, its techniques, and how it can transform your interactions, allowing you to build genuine connections and leave a lasting impression. Active listening is more than just hearing words;

it involves fully engaging with the speaker, understanding their message, and responding thoughtfully. By practicing active listening, you convey respect and interest, paving the way for deeper, more meaningful conversations.

THE IMPORTANCE OF ACTIVE LISTENING

- ✓ Building Trust: When you listen actively, you demonstrate that you value the speaker's perspective, fostering trust and openness in your relationship.
- ✓ Enhancing Understanding: Active listening helps you grasp the nuances of what's being said, allowing for better comprehension and fewer misunderstandings.
- ✓ Encouraging Engagement: By showing genuine interest, you encourage others to share more openly, creating a richer dialogue.

Before entering a conversation, take a moment to prepare yourself. Here are some key strategies:

- ✓ Clear Your Mind: Set aside distractions—both mental and environmental. Focus on the speaker and the conversation at hand.
- ✓ Adopt an Open Posture: Position your body to face the speaker, with arms relaxed and open. This nonverbal cue signals that you are receptive and engaged.
- ✓ Be Present: Commit to being in the moment. Put away your phone and resist the urge to multitask.

Once you're prepared, it's time to engage in the conversation. Here are practical techniques to practice active listening:

- Maintain Eye Contact: This shows the speaker that you are focused on them. It builds rapport and encourages them to continue sharing.

    Example: Imagine you're at a networking event, and someone is sharing their career journey. By maintaining eye contact, you convey that you're genuinely interested in their story.

- Nod in Agreement: Simple gestures, like nodding, can affirm that you are following along and understanding their points. It encourages the speaker to continue.
- Use Verbal Affirmations: Phrases such as "I see," "That's interesting," or "I understand" can reinforce your engagement without interrupting the flow of conversation.
- Avoid Interrupting: Resist the urge to jump in with your thoughts or solutions. Allow the speaker to finish their ideas before responding.

After the speaker has shared their thoughts, it's crucial to reflect and respond thoughtfully.

- Summarize Key Points:** Paraphrasing what the speaker has said demonstrates that you've been attentive and have grasped their message.

    Example: "So, what I'm hearing is that you faced challenges in your last project due to tight deadlines, but you managed to deliver successfully. That's impressive!"

- Ask Open-Ended Questions:** Engage further by asking questions that encourage deeper exploration of their thoughts. This shows your interest and invites them to share more.

Example: "What strategies did you implement to manage the project under those constraints?"

To cultivate your active listening skills, seek opportunities to practice in everyday conversations. Here are a few scenarios to consider:

- Networking Events: Use networking opportunities to engage with others actively. Approach someone and ask about their work, then practice your active listening techniques.
- Team Meetings: During team discussions, focus on listening to your colleagues' ideas and feedback. Reflect and respond to create a collaborative environment.
- Casual Conversations: Apply these skills in everyday interactions, whether with friends or family. Show interest in their stories and experiences.

As you develop your active listening skills, you'll notice a shift in your interactions. Conversations will become more enriching, and relationships will deepen. By showing genuine interest and engagement, you not only enhance your communication skills but also create a positive atmosphere that encourages collaboration and connection.

Action Steps:

1. Prepare for Conversations: Clear your mind and adopt an open posture before engaging with others.
2. Practice Active Listening Techniques: Maintain eye contact, nod, and use verbal affirmations to show engagement.

3. Reflect and Respond Thoughtfully: Summarize key points and ask open-ended questions to encourage further discussion.
4. Seek Opportunities to Practice: Use networking events, team meetings, and casual conversations to refine your active listening skills.

TAILORING YOUR COMMUNICATION TO YOUR AUDIENCE

- Cultural Sensitivity: Be aware of cultural differences in communication styles. What may be acceptable in one culture could be perceived differently in another.
- Adjusting Your Language: Use language and terminology that your audience can relate to. Avoid overly technical terms unless you are certain the audience is familiar with them.

Confidence plays a critical role in effective communication. Here are ways to build your confidence:

- Reflect on Your Communication Style: Take note of your strengths and areas for improvement.
- Engage in Active Listening: Practice active listening in your daily interactions to strengthen your connections.
- Seek Opportunities for Practice: Look for situations to practice your communication skills, whether in formal settings or casual conversations.
- Request Feedback: After conversations or presentations, ask for feedback to continuously improve.

- Positive Self-Talk:** Challenge negative thoughts about your communication abilities. Replace them with affirmations that reinforce your strengths.

Reflect on Your Communication Style: Write down your strengths and areas for improvement. Set specific goals for growth. Seek opportunities for practice: Volunteer to give presentations, join a speaking club, or participate in group discussions to refine your skills. Request Feedback. After meetings or presentations, ask a trusted colleague for specific feedback on your communication style and effectiveness.

Prepare Conversation Starters: Think of interesting conversation starters or questions that can initiate meaningful discussions with other attendees. This can include asking about their professional experiences, recent projects, or industry trends. Be genuinely interested in their responses, and actively listen to build rapport. Update Your Online Presence: Ensure that your online profiles, such as LinkedIn or professional websites, are up to date and accurately reflect your current professional achievements and goals. This will enable others to learn more about you before and after the event. Bring Business Cards: Carry a sufficient number of business cards to exchange contact information with other professionals. Ensure that your business cards are professional and include your name, job title, company, and contact details. Consider adding a brief tagline or a unique touch that reflects your personal brand.

Knowing when and how to exit a conversation is just as important as starting one. Lets discuss strategies for gracefully ending a conversation, such as expressing gratitude, exchanging contact information, or introducing the person to someone else. By ending conversations on a positive note, you'll leave a lasting impression and maintain a positive networking experience.

Exiting a conversation gracefully is a vital skill in networking. By recognizing the right moment to leave, expressing gratitude, exchanging contact information, and following up, you create a positive and memorable experience for everyone involved. Remember, every interaction is an opportunity to build relationships, and a thoughtful exit can pave the way for future connections.

Action Steps:
1. Practice Recognizing Exit Cues: Pay attention to body language and conversation flow in your interactions.
2. Use Gratitude and Contact Exchange: Incorporate expressing gratitude and exchanging information in your conversations.
3. Introduce Others: Look for opportunities to connect people you meet.

While starting a conversation is crucial, knowing how to exit a conversation gracefully is equally important. A well-timed and thoughtful exit can leave a positive impression, reinforce relationships, and encourage future interactions. In this chapter, we will explore effective strategies for concluding conversations gracefully, ensuring that you maintain a positive networking experience.

Exiting a conversation properly demonstrates respect for the other person's time and reinforces your professionalism. A positive exit can:

- Leave a Lasting Impression: A courteous farewell ensures that you are remembered fondly.

- Open the Door for Future Interactions: A graceful exit can pave the way for future connections and collaborations.
- Maintain Networking Etiquette: Knowing when to exit prevents conversations from dragging on and allows you to engage with more people.

Knowing when to exit a conversation is key to a graceful departure. Here are some cues that indicate it may be time to wrap things up:

- Body Language: Pay attention to the other person's body language. If they start to glance around the room, check their watch, or shift their posture, it might be time to conclude the conversation.
- Topic Exhaustion: If the conversation has hit a lull or the topic has been thoroughly discussed, it's a good indication that it's time to exit.
- Time Constraints: Be mindful of your schedule and the other person's. If you've been talking for a while, kindly acknowledge that you need to move on.
- Environmental Cues: Pay attention to the context of the event. For example, if people are starting to gather for a presentation or if the venue is closing, those are clear signs it's time to politely exit.

Once you've recognized the right moment to exit, use these strategies to conclude the conversation positively:

1. Express Gratitude- Thank the person for their time and insights. This shows appreciation and reinforces a positive connection.

Example: "Thank you so much for sharing your experiences with me. I really enjoyed our conversation!"
2. Exchange Contact Information- If you haven't already, now is a great time to exchange business cards or contact information. This gesture signals your interest in staying connected.

    Example: "I'd love to stay in touch. Here's my card. Let's connect on LinkedIn!"
3. Introduce Them to Someone Else - If appropriate, introduce the person to someone else at the event. This not only helps them expand their network but also allows you to exit gracefully while creating a positive impression.

    Example: "Have you met my colleague, Sarah? She works in a similar field and I think you two would have a lot to discuss!"
4. Summarize Key Points- Briefly recap any important takeaways from the conversation. This reinforces the value of the interaction and shows that you were actively engaged.

    Example: "I appreciate your insights on digital marketing trends; they have given me a lot to think about."
5. Signal the End - Use verbal cues that indicate you are wrapping up the conversation.

    Example: "As much as I'd love to continue chatting, I need to catch my next meeting."

As you prepare to exit the conversation, ensure that your tone remains positive and friendly. Here are some phrases to help you conclude:

- "It was great meeting you! I look forward to connecting again soon."
- "I really enjoyed our discussion. Let's keep in touch!"
- "Thank you for your time. I hope you enjoy the rest of the event!"

After concluding a conversation, it's essential to follow up. This reinforces your connection and shows that you value the relationship. Here's how you can do that:

- Send a Follow-Up Message: Within a day or two, send a brief email or LinkedIn message thanking them again for the conversation and mentioning something specific you discussed. This personal touch keeps you top of mind.

    Example: "Hi [Name], I just wanted to thank you again for the great conversation at the conference. I found your insights on content marketing fascinating, and I'd love to explore that further!"

- Connect on Social Media: If you haven't already, connect with them on professional social media platforms. This keeps the lines of communication open.
- Share Valuable Resources: If you came across an article or resource that relates to something you discussed, consider sharing it as part of your follow-up. This shows initiative and thoughtfulness.

To become proficient at exiting conversations gracefully, practice is key. Here are ways to hone your skills:

- Role-Playing: Practice with friends or colleagues. Take turns initiating and exiting conversations to get comfortable with different scenarios.

- Observe Others: Attend networking events and pay attention to how others exit conversations. Take notes on what works well and what doesn't.
- Set Goals: Challenge yourself to meet a certain number of new people at events and practice your exit strategies with each interaction.

Exiting a conversation gracefully is a vital skill in networking. By recognizing the right moment to leave, expressing gratitude, exchanging contact information, and following up, you create a positive and memorable experience for everyone involved. Remember, every interaction is an opportunity to build relationships, and a thoughtful exit can pave the way for future connections.

Action Steps:

1. Practice Recognizing Exit Cues: Pay attention to body language and conversation flow in your interactions.
2. Use Gratitude and Contact Exchange: Incorporate expressing gratitude and exchanging information in your conversations.
3. Introduce Others: Look for opportunities to connect people you meet.
4. Follow Up Promptly: Send a follow-up message or connect on social media after your conversation.
5. Role-Play Exiting Scenarios: Practice your exit strategies with friends or colleagues to build confidence.

The Power of Connections: A Mentee's Guide to Networking Mastery

CHAPTER 3
EXPANDING YOUR NETWORK

The greatest gift you can give someone is your time and attention." – Unknown

In today's digital age, expanding your network online is just as important as networking in person. Before attending a networking event, it's important to research and gather information about the event itself. Lets discuss the key aspects to research, such as the event's purpose, target audience, speakers, and schedule. By understanding the event's context, you'll be better prepared to make meaningful connections and engage in relevant conversations.

While online platforms have revolutionized the way we connect, attending conferences offers a unique opportunity to engage in meaningful face-to-face interactions. Conferences are not just gatherings; they are hubs of knowledge, collaboration, and inspiration. This chapter delves into the immense power of conferences and how they can significantly enhance your networking efforts online and offline

Conferences provide a plethora of benefits that can elevate your networking game:
1. Direct Access to Industry Leaders. Conferences often feature keynote speakers, panel discussions, and workshops led by industry experts. This access allows you to learn

from the best, ask questions, and gain insights that can shape your career and business.
2. Opportunities for Collaboration. Meeting peers in your field fosters collaboration and idea-sharing. You may find potential partners for projects or initiatives that can expand your reach and impact.
3. Diverse Perspectives. Engaging with diverse attendees exposes you to new ideas, trends, and practices. Embracing different viewpoints can spark creativity and innovation in your work.
4. Enhanced Credibility. Being present at a reputable conference enhances your professional credibility. It signals to others that you are committed to your field and eager to learn and grow.

Preparing for a Successful Conference Experience .Setting clear objectives for each networking event is crucial for maximizing your time and efforts. Define your objectives, whether it's meeting specific people, learning about industry trends, or seeking potential collaborations. By setting goals, you'll have a clear focus and purpose, making your networking efforts more effective.

Researching the networking event before attending is a crucial step to ensure you make the most out of the experience. Understand the purpose and theme of the networking event. Is it focused on a specific industry, skillset, or topic? Knowing the event's purpose will help you align your goals and expectations accordingly. Identify the target audience for the event. Is it geared towards professionals from a particular industry, entrepreneurs, or a broader audience? This information will help you gauge the types of individuals you can expect to meet and tailor your networking approach accordingly. By conducting thorough research on these key aspects, you will gain a better understanding of the networking event and be well-equipped to make meaningful connections and engage in relevant conversations. The more prepared you are, the more confident and proactive you can be in maximizing your networking opportunities.

Look into the speakers and panelists who will be presenting at the event. Research their backgrounds, areas of expertise, and any notable achievements. This will enable you to engage in informed conversations and seek out specific individuals whose insights or experiences align with your interests. Familiarize yourself with the event's schedule and agenda. Take note of the timing for different sessions, networking breaks, and any interactive activities. Planning your time in advance will help you prioritize which sessions or activities to attend and ensure you don't miss out on valuable opportunities.

Making the Most of Networking Opportunities. Conferences are networking goldmines. Here are strategies to make the most of these opportunities:

- Engage in Conversations: Approach fellow attendees with genuine curiosity. Ask open-ended questions and listen actively to foster deeper connections. Remember, networking is about building relationships, not just exchanging business cards.
- Participate in Workshops and Breakout Sessions. These smaller settings often encourage interaction and discussion. Take advantage of these opportunities to connect

with presenters and fellow participants in a more intimate environment.

Attending conferences is a powerful way to expand your professional network, foster collaboration, and gain valuable insights. The face-to-face interactions, diverse perspectives, and knowledge-sharing opportunities available at conferences can significantly enhance your online networking efforts. Conferences can significantly enhance your online networking efforts as well. Building an Online Community. Leverage the connections made at the conference to build an online community. Create a group or forum where attendees can continue discussions, share resources, and collaborate on projects. Showcasing Your Expertise: Participating in conferences can lead to invitations for webinars, podcasts, or online panels. Use these opportunities to showcase your expertise and further expand your network.

As you prepare for your next conference, remember the importance of setting goals, engaging authentically, and following up effectively. Embrace the transformative power of conferences, and watch as your network expands and your opportunities multiply.

Action Steps:
1. Before the Conference:
   - Set specific networking goals and identify key individuals to connect with.
   - Research the conference agenda and speakers to prepare insightful questions.
2. During the Conference:
   - Actively engage in conversations and participate in workshops.

- Use social media to connect and share your experiences in real-time.
3. After the Conference:
    - Follow up with new contacts and keep the conversation going.
    - Create content that highlights your conference insights to share with your online network.

CHAPTER 4
ONLINE NETWORKING

"Your network is the people who want to help you. It's not just about what you know; it's about who you know and how you leverage those relationships."

- Reid Hoffman, co-founder of LinkedIn

In the pervious chapter we gave you the tools to navigate through networking conferences with winning confidence . Continue the conversation online. Engage with your new contacts on social media. Share relevant articles, comment on their posts, and maintain an ongoing dialogue that fosters relationship-building. Why you ask ? , because online networking platforms, such as LinkedIn, or professional association websites, offer opportunities to connect with professionals in your industry.

We will explore how to effectively utilize these platforms to find networking events, join relevant groups, and connect with attendees. By utilizing online networking platforms, you can expand your network and discover new professional opportunities With today's digital landscape, the art of networking has transcended traditional boundaries, creating a vibrant ecosystem where professionals can connect from across the globe. Online networking is not just a trend; it's a vital skill that can significantly impact your career trajectory. This chapter will explore the transformative power of online networking and provide a narrative on how to effectively navigate this dynamic environment to achieve meaningful connections and professional growth.

As you embark on your online networking journey, envision a vast ocean of opportunities just waiting to be explored. The digital realm is teeming with professionals eager to connect, share insights, and collaborate. However, to thrive in this space, you must first craft a compelling online persona that reflects your professional identity. This involves optimizing your profiles on platforms like LinkedIn, Twitter, and industry-specific forums. A polished profile, complete with a professional photo and a captivating bio, serves as your digital business card—an invitation for others to engage with you.

Consider the story of Lisa, a recent graduate entering the competitive field of marketing. Eager to make her mark, Lisa knew she had to stand out in the crowded online landscape. She took the time to curate her LinkedIn profile, showcasing her skills, achievements, and passion for marketing. By sharing articles related to industry trends and posting her insights, she began to attract attention from professionals in her field. Her consistent engagement transformed her profile into a hub of activity, drawing connections from every corner of the marketing world. But creating an appealing online presence is just the beginning. Building meaningful relationships requires intentionality and effort. Lisa understood that networking was not merely about accumulating connections; it was about fostering genuine relationships. When she reached out to industry veterans, she personalized her messages, referencing shared interests and expressing her admiration for their work. This thoughtful approach made her outreach more impactful and opened the door to meaningful conversations.

.As Lisa navigated the online networking landscape, she discovered the immense value of participating in virtual events. She attended webinars and conferences, where she engaged with speakers and fellow attendees. During one particularly inspiring session, she connected with a panelist who shared her passion for digital marketing. After the event, Lisa followed up with a heartfelt message, thanking the panelist for her insights and expressing a desire to stay in touch. This simple gesture blossomed into a mentorship, providing Lisa with invaluable guidance as she launched her career. However, online networking is not without its challenges. Lisa initially struggled with digital fatigue as the sheer volume of online interactions began to overwhelm her. Recognizing the need for balance, she set boundaries to ensure that her networking efforts remained enjoyable and productive. By prioritizing quality over quantity, Lisa focused on cultivating deeper connections rather than spreading herself too thin.

Throughout her journey, Lisa also learned the importance of being a resource for others. She shared valuable articles, offered insights, and made introductions within her network. By positioning herself as a helpful contact, she not only solidified her relationships but also fostered an environment of reciprocity. Her connections began to seek her out for advice and collaboration, further expanding her network and influence.

As Lisa's online presence grew, she encountered individuals who inspired her with their success stories. One such story was that of David, a seasoned entrepreneur who leveraged social media to build his brand. Through consistent engagement and authentic storytelling, David attracted a loyal following that eventually led to lucrative business opportunities. Inspired by his journey, Lisa embraced her own narrative, sharing her experiences and lessons learned along the way. This not only resonated with her audience but also positioned her as a thought leader in her field.

In time, Lisa's dedication to online networking paid off. She secured internships and job offers through connections she had made, each opportunity leading her closer to her career aspirations. Her network became a powerful asset, providing insights, referrals, and support as she navigated the early stages of her career.

Winning through online networking is a journey that requires intentionality, authenticity, and resilience. By crafting a compelling online persona, building meaningful relationships, and embracing the opportunities presented by virtual events, you can unlock a world of possibilities for career growth. Remember that networking is not just about what you can gain; it's about creating a community of support, collaboration, and mutual growth. As you navigate the digital landscape, approach each connection with curiosity and a genuine desire to learn, knowing that every interaction has the potential to shape your professional journey in remarkable ways. Embrace the power of online networking, and watch as your career flourishes in ways you never imagined.

Building and maintaining relationships online requires consistent effort and genuine engagement. It is important to maintain a professional online presence while being mindful of online etiquette. By building and maintaining relationships online, you can strengthen your network and open doors to new opportunities. Online networking can significantly impact your career development. Online connections can lead to job opportunities, mentorship, collaborations, and professional growth. Developing strategies for leveraging your online network to advance your career and stay updated with industry trends once master can be utilize as the "golden ticket". By leveraging online networking for career development, you can expand your professional horizons and achieve your goals.

CHAPTER 5
MASTERING THE ART OF FOLLOW-UP

"The influence of a good teacher can never be erased."

– Unknown

Like Sara you attended several networking events, absorbing knowledge and insights from industry leaders. Now what?

Remind yourself. "I need to follow up," "That's where the real relationship begins."

In the world of networking, the initial connection is just the beginning. The true value of your network lies in the relationships you cultivate and over time. Following up is a crucial step that transforms a fleeting encounter into a lasting connection. This chapter will delve into the art of follow-up, offering strategies and techniques to help you nurture relationships, stay top of mind, and maximize the potential of your network. In networking, following up is just as important as making the initial connection. This chapter will guide you through the art of follow-up, providing you with strategies to nurture relationships, stay top of mind, and maximize the potential of your network connections.

Follow-up is not just a one-time effort; it is an ongoing process for building long-term relationships. We will explore strategies for nurturing and maintaining relationships over time, including periodic check-ins, staying updated with your network's activities, and celebrating milestones and achievements. By leveraging follow-up for long-term relationship building, you can cultivate a strong and supportive network that can provide opportunities throughout your career.

Building Trust and Credibility. Consistent follow-up demonstrates your commitment to the relationship and shows that you value the other person's time and input. This helps establish trust and credibility, which are essential for strong professional relationships.

Creating Opportunities. Following up can lead to unexpected opportunities, whether it's a job offer, collaboration, or an invitation to participate in a project. Many opportunities arise from maintaining open lines of communication. In a fast-paced environment, it's easy for connections to fade away. Regular follow-ups ensure that you remain relevant and top of mind, making it more likely that your contacts will think of you when new opportunities arise. Send a quick follow-up message within 24-48 hours of your initial meeting or conversation. This helps reinforce the connection while it's still fresh in both your minds. A simple thank-you note or message expressing appreciation for the conversation can go a long way.

Set reminders for follow-ups based on the context of your initial meeting. For example, if you discussed a specific topic or project, follow up in a week or two to share relevant resources or insights. Establish a schedule for periodic check-ins with key contacts. This could be monthly, quarterly, or even annually, depending on the nature of your relationship. Regular check-ins help maintain the connection without overwhelming your contacts. Tailor your follow-up message to reflect your conversation.

Mention specific topics discussed or insights shared to show that you were engaged and attentive. Personalization builds rapport and strengthens relationships.

Be clear and concise in your follow-up message. State the purpose of your message upfront and avoid unnecessary details. For example, "I enjoyed our conversation about digital marketing strategies at the conference. I'd love to share an article I think you'll find interesting. Include a call to action that encourages further interaction. This could be a suggestion to meet for coffee, a request for a phone call, or an invitation to connect on social media. For instance, "Would you be open to connecting over coffee next week to discuss our projects further?"

DIFFERENT FOLLOW-UP METHODS

1. Email is a versatile and professional way to follow up. Use it for more formal communications, such as expressing gratitude after a meeting or sharing resources. Ensure your subject line is engaging and relevant to capture attention.
2. Social Media, Platforms like LinkedIn and Twitter can be effective for follow-ups, especially for more casual connections. Send a connection request with a personalized note or engage with their posts to maintain visibility.
3. Phone Calls, A phone call can be a more personal touch, especially for significant connections. Use this method when you want to discuss something in-depth or if the person has expressed a preference for phone communication.

4. In-Person Meetings, If feasible, suggest an in-person meeting for a more impactful follow-up. This is particularly effective for local contacts and can help deepen relationships.

Keep your connections engaged by sharing relevant articles, resources, or insights that align with their interests or professional goals. This positions you as a valuable resource in their network. Celebrate Milestones. Acknowledge your contacts' accomplishments, such as job promotions, work anniversaries, or personal milestones. A simple message of congratulations shows that you care about their success.

MEASURING THE EFFECTIVENESS OF YOUR FOLLOW-UP

1. Track Your Interactions-Maintain a record of your follow-up interactions, noting details such as dates, topics discussed, and any commitments made. This helps you stay organized and ensures you don't miss opportunities to reconnect.
2. Evaluate Responses- Pay attention to how your contacts respond to your follow-ups. Are they engaging in conversations? Are they open to further discussions? Adjust your approach based on their level of interest and engagement.
3. Refine Your Strategy- Continuously assess and refine your follow-up strategy based on the feedback you receive and your own experiences. Experiment with different methods, timing, and messaging styles to find what works best for you.

Mastering the art of follow-up is essential for transforming initial connections into meaningful relationships. By understanding the impact of follow-up, timing your messages effectively, crafting personalized communications, and nurturing your connections over time, you can create a robust network that supports your professional growth. Remember, networking is not just about collecting contacts; it's about cultivating relationships that can lead to collaboration, opportunities, and lasting impact. Embrace the art of follow-up, and watch as your connections flourish.

Our friend Sarah can give us an insightful tactic, she continued to nurture her relationship with her mentor Mark, because of this new opportunities emerged. He introduced her to other professionals in his network, leading to valuable connections that opened doors for her career. Sarah realized that her initial follow-up had set off a chain reaction—one that not only strengthened her bond with Mark but also expanded her professional network.

Mastering the art of follow-up add another tool to your toolbox and transform your approach to networking. Follow-up is not just a task—it's an opportunity to build trust, create opportunities, and nurture relationships that can lead to remarkable outcomes.

Like Sara remember to reflected on your journey, Sara understood that networking is not merely about making connections; it's about cultivating relationships that matter. By embracing the art of follow-up, you will unlock a world of possibilities.

Action Steps:
1. Create a Follow-Up Plan:
    - Outline a plan for following up with key contacts, including timelines and methods for communication.

2. Personalize Your Messages:
   - Practice personalizing your follow-up messages based on your interactions to enhance engagement.
3. Set Reminders:
   - Use calendar tools or apps to set reminders for follow-ups, ensuring that you stay organized and proactive.
4. Evaluate Your Approach:
   - After a few follow-up interactions, assess the effectiveness of your strategy and make adjustments as needed.

CHAPTER 6
NETWORKING WITH PURPOSE

"Mentoring is a brain to pick, an ear to listen, and a push in the right direction."– John C. Crosby

NETWORKING WITH PURPOSE

Growing your network is a powerful way to create meaningful connections that can lead to personal and professional growth. By preparing effectively, and implementing strategies for engagement, you can maximize your in-person or virtual networking opportunities. Embrace the richness of interactions, and remember each conversation is a potential gateway to collaboration, mentorship, or new opportunities. As you venture into the world of networking, let your curiosity guide you, and watch as your network expands and flourishes.

Expanding your network offline is a journey that requires intention, preparation, and an open mind. By embracing the strategies and insights outlined in throughout The Power of Connections: A mentee's Guide to Networking , you can navigate the world of networking with confidence and purpose. Remember, every interaction is an opportunity to learn, grow, and connect with others who share your passions and goals. As you foster these relationships, you'll find that your network becomes a powerful resource for collaboration, support, and professional development. As you move forward, keep in mind that networking is not just about what you can gain but also about what you can offer to others. By contributing to your network, you create a cycle of generosity that will ultimately benefit you and those around you.

In the vast expanse of the professional world, networking is often viewed as a mere transactional process—a means to an end. However, when approached with intention and clarity, networking transforms into a powerful catalyst for personal and professional growth. The Power of Connections: A mentee's Guide to Networking " delves into the concept of purposeful networking, illustrating how a strategic and meaningful approach can unlock opportunities, foster collaborations, and create lasting relationships.

Imagine standing at the edge of an expansive forest, each tree representing a potential connection. While the sheer number of trees can be overwhelming, knowing your destination can guide your path. Purposeful networking is akin to having a map that directs you toward your goals, helping you navigate through the myriad of connections available.

To illustrate the impact of purposeful networking, let's reference back to the story of Alex, remember our mid-career professional. Alex understood that simply connecting with as many people as possible would not lead him to his goal. Instead, he needed to approach networking with a clear sense of direction.

Alex started by identifying key individuals in the entrepreneurial space—founders, investors, and mentors—whose experiences aligned with his aspirations. Instead of sending generic connection requests, Alex personalized each message, articulating why he admired their work and how he hoped to learn from them.

This intentional outreach established a foundation of respect and authenticity, setting the tone for future interactions.

Recognizing the power of shared experiences, Alex sought out networking events tailored to aspiring entrepreneurs. He attended workshops, pitch competitions, and industry conferences, each time approaching these gatherings with purpose. Rather than merely exchanging business cards, he engaged in meaningful conversations, asking probing questions that revealed insights about the entrepreneurial journey. Alex shared his own aspirations and the purpose behind his networking efforts. This openness forged a connection rooted in shared experiences and mutual understanding.

Alex understood that purposeful networking is a two-way street. By sharing resources, offering assistance, and connecting others within his network, he cultivated an environment of reciprocity. His willingness to support others not only strengthened existing relationships but also attracted new connections who recognized his genuine commitment to collaborative success.

Networking should be a two-way street. Avoid dominating conversations with your achievements. Instead, practice active listening and show genuine interest in others' experiences. Networking can be an excellent way to gain insights into your professional skills and areas for growth. Don't hesitate to ask for feedback from peers or industry leaders. Focus on connecting with speakers and industry leaders. Approach them after their presentations or during breaks, and make sure to reference something specific from their talk to establish relevance. Networking offers an opportunity to share knowledge and learn from others.

Participate actively in discussions and be open to learning from different perspectives. Broaden your horizons by attending events outside your immediate field. This can expose you to new ideas and trends that can influence your work positively.

As you embark on your own networking journey, remember the significance of networking with purpose. Define your objectives, identify the individuals who align with your goals, and approach each interaction with authenticity and curiosity. Embrace the power of storytelling to forge emotional connections and create lasting relationships. And, most importantly, cultivate a mindset of reciprocity, understanding that the relationships you build are not just for your benefit—they are a shared journey toward mutual success.

In a world where connections can sometimes feel fleeting, purposeful networking stands out as a powerful strategy for creating meaningful relationships that enrich your career and personal growth. Approach each networking opportunity with intention and watch as your professional landscape transforms, opening doors to possibilities you never thought possible. Embrace the journey, connect with purpose, and let your network become a thriving ecosystem of collaboration, support, and success.

CHAPTER 7

NETWORKING ETIQUETTE AND BEST PRACTICES

"The best way to find yourself is to lose yourself in the service of others".– Mahatma Gandhi

Networking etiquette plays a vital role in building and maintaining professional relationships. Approaching professionals can sometimes feel intimidating, but with the right approach, you can establish valuable connections. We will discuss techniques for introducing yourself, initiating conversations, and expressing genuine interest in others' work. Additionally, we'll explore the importance of active listening and asking thoughtful questions to foster engaging conversations. By approaching and connecting with professionals in a respectful and authentic manner, you can create a positive and lasting impression.

In the realm of professional networking, etiquette is the foundation upon which strong relationships are built. Proper networking etiquette not only helps you make a positive impression but also fosters trust and respect among peers. By adhering to best practices, you can navigate networking situations with confidence and cultivate meaningful connections that support your career growth.

Before attending any networking event, clearly define your objectives. Are you looking to meet potential clients, seek mentorship, or expand your industry knowledge? Having specific goals will guide your approach and interactions. Familiarize yourself with the event's agenda, speakers, and key attendees. This knowledge will help you identify individuals you want to connect with and provide conversation starters.

Be Mindful of Body Language. Non-verbal cues play a significant role in networking. Approach others with open and welcoming body language—maintain eye contact, smile, and present a confident posture. When introducing yourself, stand tall, offer a firm handshake (if appropriate), and maintain an approachable demeanor. Prepare a concise and engaging introduction that summarizes who you are, what you do, and what you're looking for. A well-crafted elevator pitch can spark interest and lead to deeper conversations. When conversing with others, actively listen and engage in the discussion. Ask open-ended questions to encourage dialogue and demonstrate that you value their insights.

Reminded yourself of the goal: to connect with other professionals in your field and gather insights. Engage in discussions, ask questions, and contribute to conversations. Your active participation can enhance your visibility and position you as a valuable connection. When entering a group conversation, assess the dynamics before joining. Wait for an appropriate moment to contribute, and be respectful of ongoing discussions.

- Example: If a panel discussion arises, don't hesitate to contribute your thoughts or ask a relevant question to the speakers.

After meeting someone, send a follow-up email or message within 24-48 hours. Reference your conversation and express gratitude for their time. This shows that you value the connection. Tailor your follow-up messages to reflect the specific conversation you had. Mention any shared interests or topics that came up, reinforcing your connection. Connect with your new contacts on professional social media platforms like LinkedIn. Personalize your connection request by referencing your meeting to make it more memorable.

- Example: "HI [Name], it was great meeting you at the conference! I enjoyed our discussion about emerging tech trends. I'd love to stay in touch and exchange insights."
- Example: "I'd love to hear more about your experience in the startup world, especially the challenges you mentioned regarding funding."

Authenticity is key in networking. Be yourself, and approach conversations with sincerity. People are more likely to connect with you when they sense genuine interest. Networking is a two-way street. Look for ways to offer value to your connections, whether through sharing resources, providing insights, or making introductions. Express appreciation to those who help you along the way. Whether it's a mentor, a new contact, or someone who provides guidance, acknowledging their support fosters goodwill and strengthens relationships.

Following up after networking interactions is crucial for nurturing relationships and staying top-of-mind. There are several strategies for sending personalized follow-up messages, such as thank-you notes or emails, within a reasonable timeframe. We will elaborate techniques for adding value to your follow-up communications, such as sharing relevant resources or offering assistance. By following up effectively, you can strengthen the connections you've made and lay the foundation for future collaboration.

Networking etiquette is not just about following rules; it's about fostering genuine connections and building trust. By embracing best practices in preparation, communication, follow-up, and relationship management, you can navigate networking situations with grace and confidence. Ultimately, effective networking is about creating a supportive community that benefits everyone involved. By being authentic, offering value, and showing appreciation, you'll not only build a robust professional network but also contribute positively to the careers of those around you. As you embark on your networking journey, remember that every interaction is an opportunity to learn, grow, and connect. Embrace the process, and you'll find that the relationships you cultivate today can lead to future collaborations, mentorships, and professional advancements.

Networking is more than just exchanging business cards; it's about cultivating meaningful relationships that can propel your career forward. In this chapter, we will explore essential practices for navigating networking events, building and maintaining relationships, giving and receiving referrals, and fostering diversity and inclusion within your professional network. By mastering these skills, you'll be well-equipped to navigate the networking landscape with confidence and professionalism.

- Navigating Networking Events and Conferences

    Networking events and conferences serve as vibrant marketplaces of ideas and connections. They present exceptional opportunities to meet professionals in your industry, learn from experts, and forge new relationships. However, attending these events can be daunting without a clear strategy.

- Setting Clear Networking Goals

    Before stepping into the venue, take a moment to define your objectives. Are you looking to connect with potential clients, seek mentorship, or learn about industry trends? By establishing clear goals, you can focus your efforts and make the most of your time.

- Engaging in Conversations

    Once at the event, actively engage with others. Approach people with a smile, maintain open body language, and listen attentively. Asking open-ended questions encourages dialogue and shows genuine interest in the other person's insights.

In both formal settings, such as breakout sessions, and informal gatherings, like social mixers, adapt your approach. In formal settings, focus on sharing knowledge and exchanging insights; in informal gatherings, relax and be more conversational. The key is to be present and approachable, making it easy for others to connect with you.

CHAPTER 8
GIVING AND RECEIVING REFERRALS

"Our chief want in life is somebody who will make us do what we can." — Ralph Waldo Emerson

Referrals are powerful tools for expanding your network and opening doors to new opportunities. Engaging actively in the referral are a fundamental component of effective networking, serving as a means to connect individuals and facilitate opportunities. By mastering the art of giving and receiving referrals, you can enhance your professional relationships and significantly expand your network. Referrals are based on trust. When you refer someone, you are vouching for their skills and character, which builds credibility for both the referrer and the referred. Referrals can lead to new job opportunities, partnerships, and collaborations, often opening doors that may not be accessible through traditional channels.

In the intricate web of professional relationships, referrals stand out as a powerful tool that can shape careers and catalyze opportunities. These endorsements are not merely casual recommendations; they symbolize trust, credibility, and a shared commitment to mutual success. This chapter explores the significance of giving and receiving referrals within the realms of networking and mentorship, highlighting how these exchanges can create a thriving professional ecosystem.

The exchange of referrals is a powerful, often underappreciated, mechanism for fostering relationships and creating opportunities. Referrals can act as the bridge that connects ambitious individuals with mentors, potential collaborators, or even job opportunities. Referrals are more than just recommendations; they symbolize trust and credibility. When you refer someone, you are essentially vouching for their skills, character, and potential. This endorsement carries weight and can significantly impact the recipient's career trajectory. For mentors and mentees alike, referrals can open doors to new opportunities, facilitate introductions to influential contacts, and enhance professional visibility.

Consider the story of Maya, a young professional navigating the complexities of the healthcare industry. Eager to expand her network, Maya joined several online communities where industry experts shared insights and experiences. Over time, she developed relationships with various professionals. When Maya expressed her interest in transitioning into a more leadership role, Mark recognized her potential and offered to refer her to a colleague who was hiring for a project manager position at a leading organzation. This act of referral not only provided Maya with a direct pathway to a job opportunity but also demonstrated the trust Mark had in her abilities.

Giving referrals is an art that requires thoughtfulness and intentionality. It begins with understanding your network and the strengths of those within it. Before making a referral, it's essential to know the individual you are recommending—their skills, aspirations, and the value they can bring to the opportunity at hand. Authenticity is paramount; only refer individuals you genuinely believe in, as your reputation is intertwined with your endorsements. When you provide context for the referral, describing the skills or qualities of the person being referred and explaining why the connection is valuable, you enhance the likelihood of a successful introduction.

The art of giving and receiving referrals is a cornerstone of effective networking and mentorship. By approaching these interactions with authenticity, intentionality, and a spirit of collaboration, you can create a powerful ecosystem that benefits everyone involved. Remember that referrals are not just about transactions; they are about building trust, fostering relationships, and supporting one another in achieving career aspirations.

As you navigate your professional journey, embrace the power of referrals. Be proactive in giving them, gracious in receiving them, and committed to nurturing the relationships that make these connections possible. In doing so, you will not only enhance your own career but also contribute to a thriving network that empowers others to succeed. Ultimately, the ability to connect people with opportunities is a profound gift that can elevate not just your career, but the entire community around you.

For instance, after referring Maya to his colleague, Mark took the time to follow up with both parties. He checked in with Maya to see how the conversation went and offered to provide any additional support she might need. This proactive approach not only demonstrated his commitment to her success but also reinforced the trust inherent in their professional relationship. Receiving referrals can be just as impactful. When someone offers to refer you, it's essential to respond with gratitude and openness. A referral is a form of support, and embracing it enthusiastically can lead to unexpected opportunities. To make the most of this chance, it's crucial to clarify your goals with the person making the referral. By communicating your career objectives and aspirations, you empower them to tailor their introductions to align with your interests.

There are of course techniques for giving and receiving referrals.

TECHNIQUES FOR GIVING REFERRALS

1. Know Your Network- Maintain a clear understanding of the skills, expertise, and interests of the people in your network. This knowledge allows you to make relevant referrals that align with the needs of others.
2. Identify Needs- Listen actively to understand the specific needs and challenges faced by your contacts. This helps you identify who in your network can best address those needs.
3. Make Thoughtful Recommendations- Like Maya ,when referring someone, be specific about why you believe they are a good fit. Highlight particular skills, experiences, or attributes that make the individual suitable for the opportunity.
4. Provide Context -When introducing two parties, provide context in your communication. Explain how you know each person and why you think they should connect, which can enhance the likelihood of a positive response.
5. Follow Up - After making a referral, follow up with both parties to see how the introduction went and if they need any

further assistance. This demonstrates your commitment to the connection.

TECHNIQUES FOR RECEIVING REFERRALS

1. Be Clear About Your Goals- Clearly communicate your professional goals and the types of opportunities you seek. This clarity helps others understand how they can assist you through referrals.
2. Express Gratitude - Always thank individuals who refer you. A simple message expressing your appreciation goes a long way in nurturing relationships.
3. Be Open to Feedback - When receiving referrals, be open to feedback on how you can improve your skills or presentation. This can enhance your chances of success in future opportunities.
4. Act Promptly - When referred to someone, act quickly to reach out. This shows respect for the person who made the referral and demonstrates your professionalism.
5. Share Outcomes -If a referral leads to a successful outcome, share that success with the person who referred you. This not only shows appreciation but also encourages them to continue referring you in the future.

Engaging actively in the referral process—both giving and receiving—can significantly enhance your networking efforts. By building strong relationships through thoughtful referrals and expressing genuine gratitude, you contribute to a supportive professional community. This collaborative spirit not only benefits your own career but also encourages others to participate in the network, fostering a cycle of mutual support and growth. When you come across someone who aligns with your network's needs, don't hesitate to make recommendations. Likewise, be open to receiving referrals from others. This reciprocal relationship not only strengthens your connections but also enhances your reputation as a trusted resource.

Whenever possible, reciprocate by referring others in your network. This practice builds a culture of support and collaboration, making everyone feel valued and connected. Look back at when Mark gave the referral for Maya resulting in her landing the position. Mark felt a sense of pride and fulfillment. He knew that by actively participating in the referral process, he was not only helping others but also strengthening her own network.

When being referred, ensure that your online presence is polished and reflective of your skills. A well-crafted LinkedIn profile or portfolio can serve as a vital tool in reinforcing the credibility of the referral. After receiving a referral, always express your gratitude to the individual who made the introduction. Acknowledgment fosters goodwill and encourages a culture of reciprocity, making it more likely that they will refer you again in the future.

Maya's story highlights a crucial aspect of referrals: they serve as a bridge, but it is the individual's responsibility to walk across it. When you receive a referral, it's essential to appreciate the trust placed in you by the person making the introduction. This trust is a powerful motivator—both for you to perform at your best and for the referrer to continue nurturing their network.

Giving referrals also has a ripple effect in building relationships. When you refer someone to an opportunity, you are not only facilitating a connection; you are strengthening your own network and reputation. Each successful referral enhances your credibility as a connector, making others more likely to seek your guidance and support. This creates a cycle where individuals are motivated to help one another, fostering a community rooted in collaboration and shared success.

Mentorship plays a pivotal role in the referral process. A mentor often has an expansive network and can be instrumental in helping you navigate it effectively. By leveraging their connections, they can facilitate introductions that align with your career aspirations. When a mentor refers you, their endorsement carries significant weight, enhancing your visibility and credibility in the eyes of potential employers or collaborators. Moreover, mentors can actively identify and share opportunities within their network, keeping you informed about job openings, projects, or collaborations that align with your goals.

Consider the dynamics of mentorship further. A mentor often serves as a guide, helping you navigate your career path and introducing you to valuable connections. However, mentors also benefit from these relationships. By investing in their mentees' growth, they enhance their own leadership skills and gain satisfaction from witnessing their mentees succeed. This mutual investment deepens the relationship and creates a foundation of trust that is essential for effective referrals.

The relationship between mentorship and referrals is reciprocal. As you grow in your career, consider how you can also refer your mentor or others in your network. This mutual support not only strengthens relationships but also fosters a culture of collaboration and generosity. Creating an environment where referrals thrive requires cultivating a culture of support and collaboration within your network. Encourage open communication, allowing individuals to share their goals and aspirations freely. This openness facilitates more effective referrals. Celebrating success stories that arise from referrals reinforces their value and encourages others to engage in this practice. Taking the initiative to offer referrals, even when you don't have a specific opportunity in mind, contributes to a culture of generosity and support.

The art of giving and receiving referrals is a fundamental aspect of effective networking and mentorship. By approaching these exchanges with authenticity, intentionality, and a spirit of collaboration, you can create a powerful ecosystem that benefits everyone involved. Referrals are not just about transactions; they are about building trust and fostering relationships that support one another in achieving career aspirations.

As you participate in your professional journey, embrace the power of referrals. Be proactive in giving them, gracious in receiving them, and committed to nurturing the relationships that make these connections possible. In doing so, you will not only elevate your own career but also contribute to a thriving network that empowers others to succeed. Ultimately, the ability to connect people with opportunities is a profound gift, one that can elevate not just your career, but the entire community around you.

Embrace the reciprocal nature of referrals. When you receive a referral, express your gratitude and keep the referrer informed about the outcome. This communication fosters goodwill and strengthens the relationship. If you secure the opportunity, share your success with those who supported you along the way. This acknowledgment not only shows appreciation but also serves as inspiration for others in your network. Consider how you can pay it forward. As you advance in your career, look for opportunities to refer others. By doing so, you contribute to a culture of support and collaboration. Your referrals can help others achieve their goals, just as you have benefited from the generosity of those who came before you. Cultivate your network, be proactive in identifying individuals who could benefit from your connections. Whether it's introducing a colleague to a potential employer or connecting a mentee with someone in their desired industry, each referral adds value to your network. This practice reinforces the idea that networking is not merely about personal gain; it is about creating a community where everyone thrives.

CHAPTER 9
NETWORKING IN DIVERSITY AND INCLUSION

"True mentorship transcends borders and backgrounds; it champions diversity, fosters inclusion, and empowers every voice to rise, creating a tapestry of strength where everyone can thrive."-unknown

The dynamic and multifaceted field of healthcare, the importance of diversity and inclusion in networking has never been more critical. As the healthcare landscape evolves, it is essential to recognize that diverse perspectives not only enhance patient care but also drive innovation and improve outcomes. This chapter explores how networking with a focus on diversity and inclusion can transform the healthcare sector, fostering an environment where all voices are heard and valued.

Healthcare is inherently diverse, encompassing a wide range of professionals, patients, and communities. However, this diversity is not always reflected in leadership roles or decision-making processes. When healthcare professionals—regardless of their background—come together to share experiences and insights, they contribute to a more holistic approach to patient care.

Take the story of Dr. Amina, a young physician who recognized the significance of diversity within her practice. Throughout her medical training, she noticed that many patients felt uncomfortable discussing their health concerns due to cultural differences or language barriers. Determined to change this, Amina actively sought to build a network that reflected the diverse communities she served.

Amina attended community health fairs, cultural competency workshops, and networking events focused on diversity in healthcare. At one such event, she met Carlos, a healthcare advocate from a local Hispanic community organization. Their conversation revealed the challenges faced by patients from underrepresented backgrounds, particularly regarding access to care and understanding health information. By connecting with Carlos, Amina gained insights that helped her approach her patient interactions with greater empathy and cultural sensitivity.

Networking in diversity and inclusion can facilitate mentorship opportunities that empower healthcare professionals from underrepresented groups. For example, consider the experience of Dr. Michael, a seasoned surgeon who made it a priority to mentor young medical students from diverse backgrounds. He recognized that representation matters and that many aspiring physicians faced systemic barriers in their journeys.

Through his mentorship program, Dr. Michael helped students navigate challenges such as securing internships, developing clinical skills, and building professional networks. In turn, these mentees brought fresh perspectives and innovative ideas to the table, enriching the learning environment for everyone involved. This dynamic exemplifies how diverse networking can create a ripple effect, inspiring future generations of healthcare leaders.

However, it is imperative to approach networking with a commitment to authentic engagement. Diversity in networking goes beyond simply creating a diverse list of contacts; it requires cultivating genuine relationships built on trust and mutual respect. When attending events or joining professional organizations, be intentional about reaching out to individuals from different backgrounds. Listen actively to their experiences and perspectives, and seek to understand the unique challenges they face within the healthcare system.

As you embark on your networking journey in healthcare, embrace the opportunity to connect with individuals from various backgrounds and experiences. Challenge yourself to engage with those who may bring different perspectives to the table. By doing so, you will not only expand your professional network but also help shape a healthcare landscape where diversity is celebrated, and all patients receive the compassionate, culturally competent care they deserve.

Together, let's create a healthcare environment that values diversity, promotes inclusion, and ultimately leads to improved health outcomes for all communities. By networking with intention and purpose, we can build a stronger, more inclusive healthcare system that reflects the rich tapestry of our society.

Networking in diversity and inclusion is more than just a buzzword; it is a commitment to creating spaces where everyone feels valued and empowered. When we think about the traditional networking landscape, it often reflects homogeneity, with individuals gravitating toward those who mirror their own experiences. However, true innovation and growth emerge when we intentionally seek connections that challenge our perspectives and broaden our understanding of the world.

Diversity in networking fosters creativity and innovation. Different backgrounds and perspectives challenge conventional thinking, inspiring fresh ideas and solutions. When individuals from varied experiences come together, they create a rich tapestry of viewpoints that can lead to innovative problem-solving. For organizations, this translates into a more dynamic workforce capable of addressing complex challenges and identifying new market opportunities.

Embracing diversity in networking requires a proactive approach. It starts with recognizing the importance of inclusivity in all interactions. When attending networking events, be intentional about engaging with individuals who may not share your background or experiences. This can be as simple as initiating conversations with someone who seems different from you or participating in groups that promote underrepresented voices.

It's essential to create spaces where diverse voices are heard and valued. As you build your network, consider how you can amplify the perspectives of those who may be marginalized. This could involve inviting diverse individuals to share their stories, highlighting their achievements, or creating platforms for them to showcase their expertise. By actively promoting diversity within your network, you contribute to a culture of inclusion that benefits everyone.

Today's diverse and interconnected world, networking must embrace diversity and inclusion. Building connections with individuals from various backgrounds enriches your professional network and fosters a more equitable environment. The ability to network effectively across different backgrounds and perspectives is more important than ever. Networking in diversity and inclusion (D&I) is about creating meaningful connections that reflect the rich tapestry of experiences, cultures, and ideas that individuals bring to the table. This chapter will guide you through the principles and strategies necessary to foster inclusive networking environments, ensuring that everyone feels valued and empowered to contribute.

Understanding the Importance of Diversity and Inclusion

Diversity encompasses a wide range of dimensions, including race, ethnicity, gender, age, sexual orientation, disability, and socio-economic status. Inclusion, on the other hand, is about creating an environment where all individuals feel respected, accepted, and able to express themselves without fear of discrimination or bias. When we prioritize networking in a D&I context, we not only enrich our own professional lives but also contribute to a more equitable and innovative workplace.

- ✓ Enhancing Creativity and Innovation: Diverse networks bring together varied perspectives that can spark creativity and drive innovation. When individuals from different backgrounds collaborate, they generate unique solutions and ideas that can propel organizations forward.
- ✓ Broadening Opportunities: Networking inclusively opens doors to opportunities that may have otherwise remained closed. It allows individuals to connect with a broader range of professionals, fostering relationships that can lead to mentorships, collaborations, and career advancements.

✓ Building Empathy and Understanding. Engaging with diverse individuals helps us cultivate empathy and understanding. This not only enhances our interpersonal skills but also contributes to a more respectful and harmonious work environment.

Understanding intersectionality is crucial when discussing diversity and inclusion. This concept recognizes that individuals have multiple identities that intersect and contribute to unique experiences of privilege and oppression. For example, a person may identify as both a woman and a person of color, which can influence their experiences in the workplace differently than someone who identifies solely as one or the other. When networking, be aware of the various identities individuals hold. This awareness can facilitate more nuanced conversations and help you appreciate the diverse experiences that inform their perspectives. By acknowledging intersectionality, you can create deeper and more meaningful connections.

Recognize and challenge your own biases. Understand that biases can manifest in various forms, influencing how we perceive others and engage in networking. Strive to approach every interaction with an open mind and a willingness to learn. Making a concerted effort to connect with individuals from various backgrounds. Attend events and join groups that celebrate diversity, and be intentional about including voices that are often underrepresented in professional spaces. Whether you're hosting a networking event or participating in one, strive to create an atmosphere that encourages open dialogue. Ensure that everyone feels comfortable sharing their experiences and perspectives without fear of judgment.

Use your network to uplift and support individuals from marginalized groups. This might include mentoring, sharing job opportunities, or simply championing their work within your professional circles. Develop your cultural awareness and sensitivity. Understand that cultural norms and communication styles can vary widely. Being adaptable and respectful in your interactions will foster stronger connections. By seeking out and attending networking events that prioritize diversity and inclusion you become part of the solution and not the problem. Remember these gatherings often feature speakers and panelists from underrepresented groups, providing valuable insights and opportunities for connection.

Leverage platforms like LinkedIn to connect with diverse professionals. Follow organizations and thought leaders that advocate for D&I, and engage with their content to expand your network. Get involved in initiatives that promote diversity within your industry. Whether it's through volunteer work, sponsorship, or attending conferences focused on D&I, these activities will enhance your understanding and expand your connections. When you meet someone new, follow up with a personalized message that reflects your conversation. Acknowledge their unique perspectives and express your interest in staying connected.

Networking is not just about making a single connection; it's about fostering ongoing relationships. Regularly check in with your contacts, offer support, and share opportunities that may benefit them. Cultivating diverse and equitable relationships is not just a practice; it is a commitment to creating a richer, more equitable professional landscape. By actively engaging with diverse individuals, being mindful of biases, and supporting underrepresented professionals, you can create a network that reflects the true essence of collaboration and innovation. Fostering an inclusive networking environment goes beyond simply inviting diverse individuals to events; it requires intentionality in how you create spaces for interaction. Here are some ways to enhance inclusivity. Be mindful of the language you use when networking. Avoid jargon or terminology that may alienate individuals from different backgrounds. Using inclusive language fosters a sense of belonging and encourages open communication.

Here are some practical techniques to enhance your networking in a D&I context:

1. Participate in Mentorship Programs: Many organizations and communities offer mentorship programs focused on underrepresented groups. Participating in these programs can provide valuable insights and help you build relationships with diverse professionals.

2. Engage in Active Listening: When networking, practice active listening. This involves fully focusing on the speaker, understanding their message, and responding thoughtfully. Active listening builds trust and shows respect for the other person's experiences.

3. Utilize Networking Platforms: Leverage online platforms that focus on diversity and inclusion, such as professional groups like NAHLE(The National Association of Latino Healthcare Executives), N.A.H.S.E(National Association

of Health Services Executives) and organizations dedicated to racial equity. These platforms can provide tailored networking opportunities and resources.

Fostering inclusive connections is also about influencing the broader culture within your organization or professional community. Here are ways to contribute to a culture of inclusion. Be an advocate for diversity and inclusion initiatives within your workplace. This could involve participating in committees, suggesting training programs, or supporting policies that promote equity.

Highlight and celebrate the success stories of diverse individuals in your network. Sharing these stories can inspire others and demonstrate the value of diverse perspectives. Facilitate connections between individuals from different departments or areas within your organization. Cross-functional networking can lead to innovative collaborations and help break down silos.

Research has shown that diverse teams are more innovative and perform better. By fostering diversity in your network, you contribute to a more robust organizational culture. The benefits of networking in diversity and inclusion extend far beyond personal gain. Inclusive networking builds stronger community ties, fostering a sense of belonging among individuals from diverse backgrounds. This creates a supportive network that benefits everyone involved. Engaging with diverse perspectives challenges your own assumptions and encourages personal growth. It broadens your worldview and enhances your ability to navigate complex social dynamics.

Building diverse inclusive networks is a transformative journey that requires commitment, awareness, and action. By actively fostering inclusive networking environments, embracing diverse perspectives, and advocating for underrepresented individuals, you create a rich tapestry of connections that can drive innovation and growth. As you move forward in your networking journey, remember that every connection has the potential to contribute to a more inclusive and dynamic professional environment. With the tools and strategies outlined in this chapter, you will navigate the networking landscape with confidence, fostering a strong and supportive network that champions diversity and inclusion. Embrace the power of diversity in your networking efforts, and watch as your professional relationships flourish, leading to enriching opportunities and a more inclusive community.

As you apply the strategies and techniques discussed in this chapter, remember that the impact of your efforts extends beyond your personal network. You are contributing to a more equitable professional landscape, one connection at a time. By prioritizing diversity and inclusion in your networking practices, you are not only enriching your own career but also paving the way for future generations of professionals to thrive in a more inclusive world.

CHAPTER 10
NETWORKING FOR CAREER GROWTH

"If opportunity doesn't knock, build a door." – Milton Berle

Networking is a powerful tool for career growth and advancement. In the ever-evolving landscape of professional development, networking emerges as a critical strategy for career growth. It transcends the traditional notions of exchanging business cards at events; instead, it embodies building meaningful relationships that can propel individuals toward their career aspirations.

Networking for career growth begins with a clear understanding of your goals. What do you want to achieve in your career? Whether it's securing a promotion, transitioning to a new field, or expanding your skill set, having a defined objective will guide your networking efforts. Once you identify your goals, you can strategically target the individuals and communities that align with your aspirations.

Effective networking also involves cultivating relationships over time. It's not simply about making a connection; it's about nurturing that connection. Follow up with individuals you meet, express genuine interest in their work, and offer assistance when possible. Regularly engage with your network through emails, social media, or casual meetups. This ongoing communication fosters trust and keeps you top of mind when opportunities arise. Building a diverse network is essential for career growth. Engaging with individuals from various backgrounds, industries, and experiences can offer fresh perspectives and open doors to new opportunities. For instance, Sarah met John, a successful marketing director from a different industry, who shared valuable strategies for leadership development that she had never considered. This connection not only broadened her understanding of leadership but also introduced her to potential job openings in sectors she hadn't initially explored.

Don't underestimate the power of mentorship in your networking journey. Seek out mentors who can provide guidance and support as you navigate your career path. A mentor can offer insights based on their experiences, help you identify areas for growth, and introduce you to valuable contacts within their own network. For Sarah, finding a mentor within her organization was a turning point. Her mentor not only provided career advice but also facilitated introductions to key decision-makers, significantly enhancing her visibility within the company.

Networking for career growth also requires a mindset of giving. Be willing to support others in your network by sharing resources, offering introductions, or providing feedback. This reciprocal approach not only strengthens your relationships but also positions you as a valuable connector within your industry. Sarah, for example, made it a point to help fellow marketing professionals by sharing job leads and insights she gained from her own networking efforts. This generosity fostered goodwill and led to others reciprocating when opportunities arose for her.

Embrace the power of storytelling in your networking endeavors. Sharing your journey, challenges, and successes can resonate with others and create a lasting impression. People are often drawn to authentic narratives that reflect resilience and ambition. By articulating your career aspirations and the steps you're taking to achieve them, you invite others to connect with you on a deeper level.

Networking for career growth is a proactive and intentional process that can significantly impact your professional trajectory. By setting clear goals, building diverse connections, nurturing relationships, seeking mentorship, leveraging online platforms, attending industry events, and adopting a mindset of giving, you can create a robust network that supports your ambitions.

As you undertake your networking journey, remember that growth often occurs outside your comfort zone. Embrace opportunities to connect with new individuals, share your story, and learn from others. The relationships you cultivate today will not only enhance your career but also contribute to a community where collaboration, support, and shared success thrive. By investing in your network, you are ultimately investing in your future.

Networking is not just about finding job opportunities; it's about building a supportive community that can aid in your professional journey. The connections you make can provide:

- ✓ Access to Information:
- ✓ Career Advancement:
- ✓ Skill Development
- ✓ Emotional Support

Before diving into networking for career growth, it's important to define your goals. By setting clear and actionable goals, you can focus your networking efforts and maximize your chances of success.

STRATEGIES FOR EFFECTIVE NETWORKING

Start by identifying individuals who are influential in your desired field. This could include industry leaders, peers, alumni from your school, or professionals you admire. Make a list of potential contacts and prioritize those you want to reach out to.

- Identify Key Contacts:

    Collaborative relationships often spark new ideas and solutions. When professionals from varied backgrounds come together, they can combine their expertise to address complex challenges

- Innovation

    Regularly check in with your contacts, share articles of interest, or ask for their opinions on relevant topics. This keeps the relationship active and demonstrates that you value their insights.

- Stay Engaged

    Acknowledge the help and support you receive from your network. A simple thank-you note or shout-out on social media can go a long way in building goodwill.

- Show Appreciation

    Networking for career growth is an ongoing journey that requires intention and effort. By actively building and nurturing relationships, you can unlock new opportunities, gain valuable insights, and foster a supportive community that propels you forward in your career. Embrace the power of networking as a tool for growth, and remember that the connections you make today can shape your professional future.

CONCLUSION

"The only way to do great work is to love what you do. If you haven't found it yet, keep looking. Don't settle." – Steve Jobs

"The Power of Connections: A Mentee's Guide to Networking Mastery" serves as a beacon for those seeking to navigate the intricate landscape of professional relationships. As you step forward in your journey, remember that every connection holds the potential to unlock new opportunities, inspire growth, and transform your career path. Embrace the art of networking not just as a means to an end, but as a powerful tool for collaboration and mutual success. By fostering genuine relationships and continually investing in your network, you are not just building a professional circle but creating a community that supports your aspirations and amplifies your impact. As you forge ahead, let the strength of your connections propel you to heights you once thought unattainable. The journey may be challenging, but with each interaction, you are crafting a legacy of influence, support, and shared triumphs. Your future is bright, and the connections you cultivate today will illuminate the path to your dreams tomorrow.

Throughout the chapters , we have explored the power and importance of networking in various aspects of our professional lives. Networking is not just about exchanging business cards or making connections; it is about building meaningful relationships, gaining insights, and creating opportunities for growth and success.

We covered a range of topics related to networking, including the fundamentals of networking, effective communication strategies, leveraging social media platforms, networking for career advancement, and networking for career transitions.

We learned that networking is not limited to specific industries or professions; it is a universal skill that can benefit individuals from all walks of life. Whether you are a recent graduate, a mid-career professional, an entrepreneur, or someone looking to make a career change, networking can play a vital role in your success.

Networking is not a one-time activity but a continuous process that requires effort, time, and dedication. It involves building and nurturing relationships, seeking opportunities to collaborate and learn from others, and staying updated with industry trends and developments.

We explored various strategies and best practices for effective networking, such as setting clear goals, being proactive in reaching out to others, attending industry events and conferences, joining professional associations, and utilizing online platforms to expand our network.

Additionally, we have emphasized the importance of authenticity and genuine connection in networking. Building meaningful relationships is not about collecting a large number of superficial connections; it is about fostering genuine connections based on mutual trust, respect, and shared interests.

Networking is not just about what others can do for us; it is also about how we can contribute to the network and support others in their professional journeys. By offering help, guidance, and support to others, we can build a strong network that is mutually beneficial. Networking is a vital practice for advancing one's career, extending well beyond the simple act of sharing contact details. It focuses on developing substantial relationships that can greatly affect your professional path. Recognizing the significance of networking starts with understanding that it opens doors to essential information, enhances career opportunities, fosters skill development, and provides emotional encouragement.

To network effectively, begin by pinpointing key individuals who hold sway in your desired sector. These can include industry leaders, colleagues, alumni, or professionals you respect. Creating a prioritized list of these contacts can streamline your networking efforts. Formulating a captivating elevator pitch is crucial. This succinct introduction should clearly express your identity, what you do, and your aspirations, enabling you to communicate effectively with various audiences. Utilizing social media platforms like LinkedIn and Twitter can significantly boost your networking initiatives. By sharing insightful content, participating in discussions, and connecting with individuals in line with your interests, you can broaden your professional network. Joining industry associations is another effective strategy, as these groups often host networking events and provide workshops and resources relevant to your field. Furthermore, volunteering for projects or committees can facilitate new connections while allowing you to demonstrate your commitment and skills.

Maintaining and nurturing your network is equally important as building it. After meeting new contacts, follow up with a message expressing gratitude and referencing your discussion. This action reinforces the bond and shows your appreciation. Staying connected with your network entails regular check-ins, sharing pertinent articles, and seeking their opinions on industry matters. Organizing networking events, whether casual gatherings or virtual meetings, can further solidify relationships and establish you as a valuable connector within your field. It's crucial to express gratitude for the help you receive from your network; simple gestures like thank-you notes or public acknowledgments can cultivate goodwill.

The wider implications of networking extend beyond personal development; they contribute to a collaborative culture within industries. A strong network can foster innovation, as partnerships often lead to creative ideas and solutions. Increased collaboration among diverse professionals encourages resource sharing and mutual support. Additionally, actively seeking diverse connections can enhance workplace inclusivity, leading to more comprehensive decision-making and improved overall results.

As we conclude this book, I encourage you to continue investing in your networking skills and applying the knowledge and strategies you have gained. Networking is a lifelong process that can open doors, create opportunities, and contribute to your overall success and fulfillment in your professional life. By intentionally cultivating and maintaining your relationships, you can unlock new prospects, gain invaluable insights, and establish a supportive community that propels your career forward. Embracing the potential of networking allows you to shape your professional future, underscoring that the connections you forge today can have a profound effect on your career trajectory.

Thank you for joining us on this networking journey. I hope this book has provided you with valuable insights and practical tips to enhance your networking abilities. Remember, the power of networking lies within you. Now, go out there, connect with others, and unlock your full potential!

ACKNOWLEDGMENTS

I would like to express my heartfelt gratitude to everyone who has supported me throughout this journey. To my family and friends, your unwavering encouragement and belief in my vision have been my greatest motivation.

A special thank you to my mentors, mentee's, and colleagues who have shared their wisdom and insights, helping to shape my understanding of the importance of connections in both personal and professional growth. Your guidance has been invaluable.

I am also grateful to the many healthcare professionals who generously shared their experiences and stories, enriching the content of this book. Your commitment to excellence and collaboration inspires me every day.

Lastly, to the readers of this book—thank you for your willingness to explore the power of networking. May the insights you gain empower you to forge meaningful connections that elevate your career and transform your life.

Together, let's continue to build a community of support, innovation, and shared success.

Janaya Hernandez

ABOUT THE AUTHOR

Janaya Hernandez is a seasoned healthcare professional with a wealth of experience and expertise in the field. Holding multiple advanced degrees, including a Doctorate in Strategic Leadership (DSL), an MBA, and a Master's in Healthcare Administration (MHA), Janaya combines her academic accomplishments with practical knowledge to drive impactful change in the healthcare sector.

As a Nurse by skill set , she is dedicated to improving patient care and organizational efficiency. Janaya's commitment to excellence extends beyond her professional roles; she actively contributes to the community as a board member and a mentor, guiding the next generation of healthcare leaders.

A proud veteran, Janaya brings a unique perspective shaped by her service, further enriching her approach to mentorship and leadership. As a board member across various healthcare leader organization's, she advocates for continuous improvement and collaboration within the industry.

With a passion for empowering others and a steadfast commitment to making a difference, Janaya Hernandez is a dynamic force in healthcare, inspiring change and fostering connections that lead to success.

Made in United States
North Haven, CT
27 October 2024